I0821926

A GUIDE TO COMPETITIVE GYMNASTICS

BY ERIN NICKS

SportsZone

An Imprint of Abdo Publishing
abdobooks.com

abdobooks.com

Published by Abdo Publishing, a division of ABDO, PO Box 398166, Minneapolis, Minnesota 55439.

Printed in the United States of America, North Mankato, Minnesota
042020
092020

Cover Photo: Ulrik Pedersen/CSM/Zuma Wire/Cal Sport Media/AP Images
Interior Photos: Paul Kitagaki Jr./Sacramento Bee/Tribune News Service/Getty Images, 4–5; Amy Sancetta/AP Images, 6; Daniel Maurer/AP Images, 9; Ulrik Pedersen/CSM/Zuma Wire/Cal Sport Media/AP Images, 11; iStockphoto, 13; Shutterstock Images, 14, 19; Iakov Filimonov/Shutterstock Images, 16; Laurence Griffiths/Getty Images Sport/Getty Images, 21; Andrew Chin/Zuma Wire/ZumaPress.com/Cal Sport Media/AP Images, 22; Melissa J. Perenson/Cal Sport Media/AP Images, 25; Jaime Lopez/Jam Media/Getty Images Sport/Getty Images, 26; Amy Sanderson/Cal Sport Media/AP Images, 28

Editor: Charly Haley
Series Designer: Megan Ellis

Library of Congress Control Number: 2019954410

Publisher's Cataloging-in-Publication Data

Names: Nicks, Erin, author.
Title: A guide to competitive gymnastics / by Erin Nicks
Description: Minneapolis, Minnesota : Abdo Publishing, 2021 | Series: Gymnastics zone | Includes online resources and index.
Identifiers: ISBN 9781532192364 (lib. bdg.) | ISBN 9781098210267 (ebook)
Subjects: LCSH: Gymnastics--Juvenile literature. | Gymnastics--Tournaments--Juvenile literature. | Sports--History--Juvenile literature. | Gymnastics for children--Juvenile literature.
Classification: DDC 796.44--dc23

CONTENTS

CHAPTER 1

WINNING GOLD

It was August 2008 at the Olympic Games in Beijing, China. Balance beam, the final event in women's gymnastics, was underway. Shawn Johnson of the United States was warming up in a separate gym. She felt awful. Her stomach was hurting, and she had a headache. Johnson's coach, Liang Qiao, tried to motivate her. He reminded Johnson that this

Shawn Johnson competes on the balance beam during the 2008 Olympics in Beijing.

Johnson, *left*, and teammate Nastia Liukin are awarded their Olympic medals.

could be her last chance at a gold medal in an individual event at these Games. Johnson left the warmup gym and headed to the main venue.

Sixteen-year-old Johnson had already clinched silver medals in the floor exercise, team competition, and the all-around event. She lost the all-around gold to her teammate, Nastia Liukin. Johnson had been the favorite to win that event. She had come so close. Johnson badly wanted a gold medal of her own.

People in the Olympic crowd were on the edges of their seats to see Johnson perform on balance beam. All of Johnson's years training as an elite gymnast had led up to this moment. She took her place at the end of the beam. Then she took a deep breath and began her routine. She showed strength and skill that had come from countless hours of perfecting each move. Johnson finished the routine with a difficult dismount. She completed the roundoff with a full-twisting double-back. Then she flashed a huge smile. She received a score of 16.225. Johnson had finally won her gold medal.

COMPETITION AT EVERY LEVEL

Johnson began in gymnastics when she was only three years old. When Qiao met her a few years later, he saw that Johnson was very talented. The two of them worked together for more than

10 years. They trained at a gym in Johnson's hometown of Des Moines, Iowa. As Johnson improved, she competed at higher levels. By the time she was 16, she was ready for the Olympics.

Competitive gymnastics includes many levels. The level at which a gymnast competes depends on his or her skill, age, and experience. Gymnasts need to pass through many different levels in order to compete at the Olympics.

There are many different competitive gymnastics events around the world. Young athletes can compete in local events. Other events are bigger, such as collegiate meets,

BABY GYMNASTICS

Gymnastics classes for babies and toddlers are available in many places. The babies learn simple skills, like bouncing on a trampoline.

Johnson won the gold medal for floor exercise at the 2007 World Championships in Stuttgart, Germany.

state and national championships, or the World Championships. These different levels prepare athletes to become Olympic hopefuls. They also help to grow the sport of gymnastics around the world.

CHAPTER 2

LEVELS OF GYMNASTICS

Becoming a competitive gymnast involves many steps. This keeps gymnasts very busy, spending many hours in the gym. Competitive gymnastics is a big commitment, and dedicated gymnasts may have to give up a lot of things that are important to them, such as enjoying time with their friends and family. Instead, they spend that time training.

There are 10 levels in the US Junior Olympics program for both men and women. These levels

Simone Biles's floor routine helped Team USA win the team gold medal at the 2019 World Championships in Stuttgart, Germany.

help gymnasts learn different skills. The skills become more difficult as the levels become higher. The programs also prepare gymnasts for competitive meets.

THE WOMEN'S PROGRAM

In the women's Junior Olympics program, Levels 1, 2, and 3 consist of recreational steps. It is a time to learn the basics. Girls learn how to perform skills like cartwheels, forward and backward rolls, and splits. Any competition comes by testing against other gymnasts at the club. A girl must be at least four years old to start at Level 1.

When a girl has completed the first three levels, she can move on to the first competitive level. The skills through Levels 4 and 5 are more difficult. The gymnast performs forward handsprings on the vault. She completes handstands and cartwheels on the balance beam. She does back handsprings and back

Gymnasts must train hard and learn new skills to advance to a competitive level.

tucks during the floor exercise. These levels allow gymnasts to compete in events such as the USA Gymnastics State Championships.

Levels 6 through 10 consist of bigger combinations of difficult moves. Girls have to be at least seven years old to compete in Level 6. By Level 8, they can compete in regional championships. When they perform their routines at meets, they have to get a minimum score before moving on to the next level. They also have to be old enough. A Level 10 gymnast has to be at least nine years old. From there she can move on to become an elite competitor.

A gymnast performs on balance beam.

THE MEN'S PROGRAM

The men's program involves three stages and 10 levels. The first stage is the Essential Elements Program. It covers Levels 1 through 3. This is where the basic skills are learned. Sometimes the boys learn the skills in a circuit or through an obstacle course. They will learn about the different types of apparatus, such as the vault, pommel horse, and high bar.

The second stage is the Age Group Competition Program, which comprises Levels 4 through 7. A boy must be at least six years old to compete in Level 4. The competitions in this stage are either the Junior Olympic Division (Division I) or the Junior Development Division (Division II). Division I is for gymnasts who want to focus on learning more skills to compete at higher levels. Division II is for gymnasts who want to compete but also enjoy more recreational gymnastics time.

A boy practices with his trainer on the pommel horse.

The third stage is the Junior National Team Program, Levels 8, 9, and 10. Boys are selected from this stage to join the Elite Program. This program is for male gymnasts who wish to continue competing beyond the Junior Olympics Program. They can go on to compete for spots on the US National Team.

CHAPTER 3

KEEPING SCORE

There are a lot of rules in both men's and women's competitive gymnastics, and many of these rules affect how gymnasts' routines are scored. It is up to a coach to teach a gymnast these rules, and the athlete has to remember all of them. Points can be deducted from routines for many reasons. Rules dictate how gymnasts approach and dismount from every apparatus. There are even rules about staying within the border of the mat during the floor exercise.

The top score a gymnast can receive depends on the level of competition. In the Junior

Competitive gymnastics is scored differently at different levels.

13

Olympics Levels 7 and 8 for women, the top score is 10. Gymnasts at that level have special requirements that they have to perform on each apparatus. If they leave out one of these requirements, they are deducted half of a point. More deductions lower the gymnast's score. But a gymnast who gets no deductions ends with the top score of 10.

For Level 9, the gymnast begins each routine with a score of 9.7 instead of 10. For Level 10, it's 9.5. However, at these levels, points can be given for more difficult moves, which means the athlete could still end up with a score of 10. When rules are broken, points are deducted.

Men's scoring at the Junior Olympics level is based on the Code of Points from the International Gymnastics Federation (FIG). This system gives gymnasts a certain amount of points for each skill they complete.

CODE OF POINTS

The FIG Code of Points is a rulebook used by the judges of male and female gymnasts. The Code of Points allows judges to award points for skills and to take deductions for mistakes. In the FIG Code of Points, skills are labeled with different letters. A very simple skill would be considered an "A."

More complicated skills, including

Biles is known for her daring performances. She has a balance beam move named after her.

Gymnasts must compete in a specific uniform or they will lose points.

dismounts, are given letters further along in the alphabet. For example, performing a full turn on the balance beam is rated an "A." When US National Team member and Olympic champion Simone Biles pulled off a triple-twisting double backflip at the World Championships in 2019, her move was awarded a "J." Before Biles' amazing performance on floor exercise that day, no other gymnast had been awarded a difficulty rating higher than the letter "I."

CLOTHING

A gymnast's appearance and clothing also affects his or her score. Men's Junior Olympics Levels 6 to 10 require all competitors to wear long pants during the pommel horse, still rings, parallel bars, and high bar. Any uniform violation earns a deduction of 0.3 points. Coaches also have to follow a dress code. They must wear a collared shirt with pants. No shorts or hats are allowed.

Women gymnasts in Levels 9 and 10 at the East/West and National Championships must wear a competition number on their uniform at all times. If they don't, they will be deducted points for a uniform violation.

CHAPTER 4

THE ROAD TO THE OLYMPICS

Gymnasts who want to continue competing after Level 10 need to become part of the Elite Program. The Elite Programs for both men and women are broken into junior and senior categories. For the men, a gymnast must be between the ages of 12 and 18 to compete in Junior Elite. Junior Elite competitions only take place in the United States. Gymnasts must be at least 16 if they want to compete around the world as a Senior Elite. For women, Junior Elites have to be between the ages of 11 to 15.

Junior Elite gymnasts continue to learn new skills. This prepares them for the international events at the next level.

US gymnast Cameron Bock won a bronze medal on the parallel bars at the 2019 Pan American Games in Lima, Peru.

Senior Elites have to be at least 16 years old. The men are selected for Elite Programs by the USA Gymnastics Men's Program Committee. Women earn their way into elite status by competing at qualifying events, such as the American Classic and the US Classic.

THE NATIONAL TEAMS

For any competitive gymnast, making the national team is a huge goal. The men's and women's national teams compete for the United States at major gymnastic events such as the World Championships and the Pan American Games. A dozen or more women from the final all-around event at the US Championships earn a spot on the national team. New members of the men's team are picked from the best at the US championships and Winter Cup.

However, before a gymnast can compete on the biggest stage in the athletic world, they

AWESOME OHASHI

College gymnastics is another way for gymnasts to compete at a high level. Katelyn Ohashi competed for the University of California, Los Angeles. Video of her floor routine at the Collegiate Challenge in 2019 went viral. She scored a perfect 10.

Members of 2016 Team USA pose after their performances at the US Olympic Team Trials, which earned them a spot in the Olympics that year.

have to clear one final hurdle. All gymnasts hoping to qualify for the Olympic Games must compete in Olympic trials. The number of athletes allowed on the team is decided by the International Gymnastics Federation. Because of the limited size of Olympic teams, most members of the national teams do not compete at the Olympic Games.

Being a part of competitive gymnastics is a rewarding experience. But it can also be a long and difficult road. Gymnasts have to commit a lot of time and energy trying to be the best. They may get injured. They may also miss out on fun childhood experiences. It takes a lot of effort for athletes to devote themselves to the sport. Despite the risks, it can be worth it for the chance to stand on top of an Olympic podium.

GLOSSARY

CIRCUIT

A series of exercises performed one after another.

DEDUCTION

When points are taken off of a gymnast's score.

DISMOUNT

To land after performing on the vault, pommel horse, balance beam, high bar, uneven bars, rings, or parallel bars.

ELITE GYMNAST

A gymnast who has completed all 10 levels of the USA Gymnastics Junior Olympics program.

HANDSPRING

An acrobatic jump through the air onto one's hands followed by springing onto one's feet.

INTERNATIONAL GYMNASTICS FEDERATION (FIG)

The sports organization in charge of governing international gymnastics, also called Fédération Internationale de Gymnastique in French.

POMMEL HORSE

An event in which male gymnasts balance and perform tricks on their hands on a bench covered with foam, rubber, and leather that has two plastic handles on the top (the pommels).

MORE INFORMATION

BOOKS

Kawa, Katie. *The Science of Gymnastics*. New York: PowerKids Press, 2016.

Lawrence, Blythe. *The History of Gymnastics*. Minneapolis, MN: Abdo Publishing, 2020.

Schlegel, Elfi, and Claire Ross Dunn. *The Gymnastics Book: The Young Performer's Guide to Gymnastics*. New York: Firefly Books, 2018.

ONLINE RESOURCES

To learn more about competitive gymnastics, please visit abdobooklinks.com or scan this QR code. These links are routinely monitored and updated to provide the most current information available.

INDEX

ABOUT THE AUTHOR

Erin Nicks is from Thunder Bay, Ontario, Canada. She has written about sports for newspapers and websites for 20 years. She currently lives in Ottawa, Ontario.